AN

EXTRAORDINARY

RELATIONSHIP

Enjoying the benefits of equality with your partner

Leo Ryan

First ebook edition: Sydney 2016
Publisher: Sydney School of Arts & Humanities
15-17 Argyle Place Millers Point NSW 2000
www.ssoa.com.au
An Extraordinary Relationship
ISBN 978-0-9954219-1-2 ebook
ISBN 978-0-9954219-0-5 print book

Cover design by Ferdinando Manzo. Text design by Ferdinando Manzo. Typeset in Times New Roman. Printed and bound by Lightning Source as a POD paperback.

National library of Australia Cataloguing-in-Publication data: Ryan, Leo, author.

An Extraordinary Relationship / Leo Ryan.
Non-fiction – How-to book – relationships

Dedication

To my partner, Gunilla,

with whom I have had an extraordinary relationship.

Acknowledgements

I owe a great debt of gratitude to Kathleen Garofali, without whose urging this book may never have eventuated. Over many years numerous people who have become aware of my work have insisted I write a book. A great supporter was my friend Michael White (1948-2008) who was world renowned for his development of 'narrative therapy'. His books have been translated into ten languages. I'm also grateful to all those who were part of a group of counsellors in the early 1980s in Adelaide. We would meet on a monthly basis to hone our skills, and then share them with others by means of workshops, talks, and seminars by invitation in many parts of Australia, Special mention is reserved for my colleague, Rob Hall, with whom I conducted the first group in Australia for men who were abusive in their relationships.

Author biography

Leo Ryan has been a counsellor for the major part of his working life. Early in his career he became aware of the number of female clients who were being abused by their husbands/partners/boyfriends and was determined to help. This book highlights his conclusions, showing it is possible for most people to bring on the changes needed to have a great relationship. Married for over thirty years, Leo has a son and daughter, his wife, Gunilla, has a daughter, and they have seven grandchildren. Leo gained a social work degree from Flinders University, has worked in Adelaide and Canberra, and now lives in Sydney.

Contents

Introduction

I'm going to share with you how to have the kind of relationship you might not realise is possible: a partnership based on harmony, friendship, intimacy and freedom. Hopefully, you will learn how to share your life with another person and have not only good communication, peace, joy and humour, but also great sex, mutual respect, confidence, trust and loyalty. In other words, you will discover how to have a relationship beyond your wildest dreams.

You'll learn to avoid the hazards many people have in their relationships and married lives, and also how to enjoy life with ease and no restraints while being a role model to others. Having an extraordinary relationship will help make your life richer, as well as more pleasurable and satisfying.

Your children will benefit immensely from their observation of the way you lead your life. The shared parenting they receive will have a major impact on them. It will affect how they live, making them more confident and caring. They will have high self-esteem, great attitudes and will live life to the fullest. Later in life, their children will follow *their* example ... and so on and so on. A revolution will occur. Lives will be transformed.

If you find this hard to believe, you need to read on – because many people do live this way, and the time has come when you may need to open up your mind and your life. Then you can enjoy with a partner the change in views that can arise – and the harmony you'll to come to understand to live more fully day by day.

Chapter 1
Why I Am Sharing

My purpose for sharing these thoughts is that there are many people who have no idea how to have a genuine connection with a partner or spouse. Countless couples are not satisfied in their relationships, but it is often not obvious why this is so. I will be outlining options that will offer solutions.

There are many books available purporting to offer solutions for the issues people have in relationships. Approaches range from making compromises and working on communication techniques, to being more accepting of perceived differences between the sexes. But I will not be covering these strategies in my explanations. I'm offering a broader approach.

Many women have given up on relationships, often after having the same unsatisfying type of experience with different men – or they rationalise a situation, deciding 'That's just the way men are' or 'I'll have to accept it'. Others keep searching in vain, hoping the next relationship will be different.

Meanwhile, we hear so much about men being confused about how to behave in a relationship. In previous generations this perhaps seemed very clear for most. Now the picture is more blurry.

What I have to say will offer a win/win for women and men alike.

Chapter 2
My Background

I was a counsellor for twenty years. During that time, I saw a broad range of clients dealing with a variety of issues. But one pattern stood out: the high number of women experiencing various forms of abuse.

This was something I had not come across before. I was surprised how common it was.

I came to realise this was an issue most people did not want to know about – an issue that covered incidents often dismissed as 'domestics' that were no one else's business.

The abuse was frequently trivialised, and views were expressed that suggested that the women deserved it or brought it upon themselves in some way.

I recall my mother saying to me: 'What's a man supposed to do if a woman spends all his money?'

As time went on, I began to suspect that if things were going to change, we had to deal with the men. As it happened, I soon discovered I had a colleague working in another location who was thinking exactly the same way.

We decided to run group counselling sessions for men who were abusive in their relationships. It was the early 1980s, and this was the first time anything like this had been done in Australia.

Consequently, we got a lot of media attention. I was interviewed on several TV and radio programs, and articles appeared in newspapers.

As time went on, I became involved with more groups. In addition, I was one of several counsellors who began running workshops to teach others in my field about the problem and how to deal with it.

I gave many talks and seminars to a range of people in the community, including doctors, nurses, police officers, church members and politicians.

While doing this, I continued to counsel men who were abusive to their partners, and I also kept working with women who were being abused. During this time, I saw many couples where the man was being abusive in various ways.

Chapter 3

Hindrances to Having Extraordinary Relationships

Abuse is one of the hindrances so let's look into that, for a start.

The issue of men abusing women in relationships was addressed publicly and broadly in Australia in the 1970s. Before then, it received very little attention. Generally, I have found that it is an experience that women deal with through the support of other women who have been abused.

To this day there has been very little progress in addressing this problem overall.

It is far more common than most people realise. The statistics of domestic violence are astounding.

Beverly Engel, an authority on the problem in the US, tells us in her keynote address at the 'Truth About Violence Against Women' conference held in Sydney in 2008 that, 'Nearly one third of American women (31 percent) report being physically or sexually abused by a husband or boyfriend at some point in their lives. Three in four women (76 percent) who reported they had been raped and/or physically assaulted after the age of eighteen said a current or former husband, cohabiting partner, or date, committed the assault.'

On average, in the United States more than three women each day are murdered by their husbands or boyfriends, according to figures compiled by the American Psychology Association. (http://edition.cnn. com/2013/12/06/us/domestic-intimate-partner-violence-fast-facts/)

In Australia, one woman is killed every week as a result of intimate partner violence. (www.whiteribbon.org.au/white-ribbon-importance)

Today, domestic violence still provides the single biggest threat of physical injury to women – even more than the *combined* threat of heart attacks, cancer, strokes, car accidents, muggings and rapes.

Statistics tell us that the most dangerous place for a woman is in her own home – not in a dark alley or in some seedy neighbourhood. We now know that, worldwide, at least one woman out of every three has been beaten, coerced into sex or otherwise abused in her lifetime, according to the UN High Commissioner for Human Rights, Navi Pillay. (www.un.org/apps/news/story.asp?NewsID=33971)

'Honour' killings are on the rise across the world, according to the United Nations, with as many as five thousand women and girls each year being murdered by members of their own families – many for the 'dishonour' of having been raped, often by a member of their own family. (www.un.org/apps/news/story.asp?NewsID=33971)

It is often thought that abuse in relationships only occurs within certain categories of people. As if it is a lower or working class issue. But that's not the case, and that's why it is important to emphasise that domestic violence occurs across all classes, sectors and cultures.

About a decade ago a local paper on Sydney's north shore ran an article indicating that one in three women in the area had been domestically abused – a statistic that may surprise some readers, as the North Shore is regarded in Sydney as a middle and upper-class enclave.

About the same time, I was the guest speaker at a women's group in this very area. The group was made up of about thirty well-to-do, impeccably dressed women. They arrived in their smart cars, and the meeting was in a big house, easily catering for the number of people present. The women's husbands, mostly, would have been successful businessmen. My subject was 'The Subtle Aspects of Abuse in Relationships', and covered put-downs, criticisms, regular fault-finding and blaming.

I had everyone's full attention. The group became very quiet; you could have heard a pin drop. Their silence revealed a lot. I'm sure many of the women related to what I was talking about – although I assumed they probably would not have thought about it from a wider perspective before, nor would they have spoken to anyone about the subject.

After my talk, at least half a dozen women indicated they wanted to come to see me as clients. I gave them my contact details, but I did not hear from any of them.

I was not surprised by their lack of contact. I imagine there would have been a denial of the reality afterwards. They would continue to live this way, and think there was too much at stake to face up to what was happening in their lives.

After all, he is such a good provider, and others think so highly of him he is like a shining knight. How is anyone going to believe he is not the person they experience?

This can be a stumbling block. Often others experience the charm of this wonderful man who can't do enough for people outside the home.

It reminds me of a man I saw as a client who was very involved in his church. He did great deeds for people in that community and they thought he was tremendous.

With his family, he was very different. In the home he was an ogre, and very abusive to his spouse and other family members.

I remember his partner being distraught and at the end of her emotional 'tether'. She told the person in charge of that church what was happening and he referred the man to me.

I made no progress with this man. I believe this was because it was not his choice to come and see me, and he refused to acknowledge that there was a problem.

Eventually the woman left him, and was happy and relieved when she did.

At a later stage, I was asked by the church leader to come and speak to the congregation about this issue. Before I spoke, the leader insisted on sharing with me the congregation's beliefs about marriage, and I told him I would not support those views in my talk. I'll let you know later the outcome of my talk, when we reach the section on what I see as the problem and the solution.

In 2009 a book about a domestic murder called *Silent Death* was published. Written by Melbourne journalist Karen Kissane, the story is about a woman named Julie Ramage who was murdered by her husband, Jamie. *Silent Death* follows Jamie's trial.

The blurb on the back cover of the book states that: 'Julie and Jamie Ramage were the classic middle-class Australian couple. They appeared to have it all: good looks, a nice home and children in private schools. But Julie walked out of their seemingly perfect marriage. And then Jamie killed her.'

Silent Death highlights many things, including the fact that a seemingly perfect life can be a façade. Julie was abused physically, sexually and in many other ways during the twenty-three years of the marriage. She was raped on a daily basis. The book also demonstrates that women are disadvantaged in relation to the law, at least in Victoria, where Jamie was charged with manslaughter, not murder, on the basis that Julie provoked him by leaving. As manslaughter is regarded as a lesser crime than murder, Jamie received a prison sentence of eleven years, with eight years before he could be released on parole.

Another case of domestic violence of which you may be aware, and one that received no shortage of publicity, involved the Australian actor Matthew Newton, who in 2010 had an Apprehended Violence Order taken out against him by a partner. (http://www.news.com.au/entertainment/tv/matthew-newton-rachael-taylor-in-hotel-lobby-fight-withdraws-channel-seven-show-x-factor/story-e6frfmyi-1225908632404)

The American performer Tina Turner offers another well-known example. Tina was abused by her partner Ike, in a variety of ways, over a long period. And when Tina finally got away from her abuser, she was left with nothing.

'Onstage Ike and Tina soared, but offstage she suffered through his violent attacks. One night in 1976, after arriving in Dallas to begin a tour, he beat her bloody en route to the hotel. As soon as he fell asleep, Tina put on sunglasses to disguise her bruised face and escaped with 36 cents in her pocket. She found refuge in a nearby Ramada Inn, then fled to Los Angeles.' (www.oprah.com/omagazine/oprahs-interview-with-tina-turner)

I watched a program on the Australian Broadcasting Commission television program, *Compass*, in which the well-known Irish author Edna O'Brien was interviewed. She talked about her marriage to fellow author, Ernest Gebler, and how he was like a tyrant in the way he treated her. (http://www.abc.net.au/compass/s4502668.htm)

This brings me to another pattern that I have noticed throughout my counselling work. Often, when people are well-off the man is in charge of the couple's finances, which the woman is unable to access. She gets used to a lifestyle where money is no object, but will have no access to the lifestyle or money if she is to leave. The woman becomes trapped. I find when talking to people about this subject most have a story to share about someone they know. At a meeting recently, a woman mentioned a friend of hers who is in an awful situation. She said her friend told her she is staying with an abusive partner because she does not want to lose her house.

When dealing with the notion of 'abuse' in relationships, we have to look at the term very broadly. The spectrum ranges from physical and sexual abuse, to mental, psychological and verbal abuse. It includes threats to harm or kill, which is a syndrome not uncommon in a lot of relationships. Women are often threatened that they will be killed if they leave – and many are. Just think back to Julie Ramage. So, such a threat is overwhelming and women become very afraid, as this could happen to them.

As a matter of fact, some men even kill the child or children after the separation as a way of retaliating because the woman left.

Three such situations spring to mind. One involved a man, whose wife had left him, having access to their three sons one Father's Day. The man deliberately drove his car into a dam with the boys inside, and all of the boys drowned. The father claimed it an accident, but he was found guilty of murdering the children (https://en.wikipedia.org/wiki/Robert_Farquharson)

Another situation in Alabama involved a father who threw his four young children into a river from a bridge. The four children drowned. They ranged in age from four months to three years. (http://www.fox-news.com/story/2008/01/09/police-man-throws-4-kids-off-bridge.html)

And in Victoria in 2014 a separated father killed his son in front of onlookers during a cricket training session at a ground south-east of Melbourne – an horrific event which later that year led to the establishment of the Luke Batty Foundation with the goal of raising funds to support women and children affected by the trauma of family violence. (http://www.abc.net.au/news/2014-02-13/mother-in-shock-after-son-killed-by-father-at-cricket-oval/5258252)

Hearing about these cases can have a big negative impact on women who might be in dreadful situations but are scared to leave, as they begin thinking something similar might happen to their children. Other people can be confused and find it difficult to understand why women stay when they are experiencing terrible abuse. They do not realise what could happen if these women do leave.

After violent episodes, a common occurrence is for men to apologise to women, and to promise they will never behave badly again. Even though the abuse has happened many times before, women can think 'this time it is different,' and that the man really means it. When the women leave, they are often pursued relentlessly. If their phone number is known, they can be called numerous times. The men will say sorry, and promise to never hurt them again, then beg to come back and be given another chance. In other words, the men will promise to do anything the women want.

Prior to women leaving, counselling will have been suggested. Some men will now agree to this as a way of winning a partner back. I have seen many men in these circumstances, and the outcomes have been poor. It is not surprising, as they are not motivated to change. It is simply a ploy to get the women to come back. I recall one occasion when I agreed to see a couple in their home. The woman had left but agreed to come to the home for a session at the man's request. When I arrived, the man was there but not the woman. On the sideboard was a magnificent vase of flowers. The woman did not come. I remember the man saying that he had wasted all that money on the flowers. Obviously he had bought them as a way of persuading her to come back.

Over time, I observed many occasions where flowers were used as a means to get women to come back, or to forgive the men. They were never being given simply as an expression of love. I saw a lot of women who had a negative reaction to receiving flowers, as the flowers had often been used as a way of manipulating them. Aside from using flowers, some men also pressure other people, such as friends and family, to coax women to come back. Those who are not aware of the dynamics of an abusive relationship can easily be persuaded to comply with these requests.

People can be influenced by the apparent remorse, or by the charm that can be displayed. Sometimes women's accounts are then doubted. This can even happen with a woman's own family. Relatives can be deceived, as the abuse may never have been witnessed, and people often doubt what the woman has to say. Also, when some women indicate that they may leave, it is not uncommon for the men to tell them they will make sure the women don't get the children. This can scare women and prevent them from leaving.

With many couples, the men are described as having bad tempers. It is often added that they never get violent. Others are referred to as being moody, with the same qualification. In such cases, the atmosphere of the home is affected, so that one always has to be on one's guard. I recall my son telling me about the father of one of his early girlfriends. He told me how moody the father was to the extent his daughter avoided being home as much as possible. He added, 'He's not violent or anything.' He also said how sorry he felt for the girl's mother.

Many excuses are made, the main one being, 'That is just how these men are and you have to accept it and make allowances.' Often it is added that the men are just like their fathers, as if this cements the case and there is nothing that can be done about it. Boys are often described this way as well. A lot of men are described as having problems with anger. It is thought they are not able to control it. This has been recognised as an issue, and these days anger management groups have proliferated. I don't believe these groups are helpful, and I will shed light on this when I come to my conclusion of Chapter 6, making clear what I think the problem is and the best approach to overturning the problem.

There are other incidents that are not directed at a woman personally, that are also acts of abuse. Such actions as slamming doors, punching holes in walls and doors, throwing objects, overturning tables and so on. The scene in the movie *Titanic*, in which Cal upends the table, is a good example of this. The consequence for Rose is that she is petrified. Generally, the outcome of these activities is that women are terrified. They have no idea what is likely to happen next. They live in fear.

Often women believe they have contributed in some way, usually because of what has been said to them by their partners. Consequently they live their lives walking on eggshells, hoping to avoid any further incidents. Mostly, men don't give any thought to how women feel, and are not at all concerned about this. Within the home, a lot of women are regularly undermined, dismissed and put down. Their capacity to do a whole range of things is questioned. Many women who hold significant positions in their workplaces are treated this way at home.

A comment one hears regularly from women is: 'He never listens to me.' They also say many men have no idea about feelings. I will examine how all this fits in later.

I recall a man I saw as a client. He was devastated because his partner had left him. He wanted to know how I could help him. I suggested a good place to start would be if I had some idea why she left him. It took some time to establish he had been abusive to her over a long period of time. After going through a whole process with him, we looked at how she would have felt, and why she would have left.

When he first came in he was totally focused on himself, with no thought of how she could have been feeling. When I was able to get him to put himself in her position, he could understand why she had left. Finally, he agreed that if he had been in her position, he would have acted the same way. He became more understanding and accepting.

Chapter 4
Other Hindrances to Consider

We also need to consider domestic and parental responsibilities.

Study after study indicates overwhelmingly that women do the bulk of the work on the home front, including parenting. This imbalance amounts to abuse as well, and must be included as part of the issue.

When abuse in relationships is mentioned, people think of the extremes, such as physical violence. Other types of abuse are usually not considered.

These types of omissions contribute to the lack of progress in addressing the issue, which becomes marginalised, and we only associate it with certain groups and categories within the community. The broader community stays removed from these 'deviant' people, denying any association at all.

These days there is an attitude that there has been a change. There is a view that women can do whatever they want, and things are much more even on the home front. This period of time has even been referred to as the post-feminist era. It is as if all the reforms of the 1960s and 1970s are firmly in place, therefore the problem is solved. Nothing could be further from the truth; there is a long way to go.

Women who work full-time on average earn eighty per cent of their male colleagues' salaries. Little has changed over the past decade since it was reported that only one in ten top executives is a woman. (Andrew West. The Sydney Morning Herald. Jan 25, 2008) And, as already stated, research shows women still bear the brunt of the burden on the home front.

Regardless, some will dispute this. The argument will be that many men are involved with their children and in the running of the household. For some men this is true, and even more so in recent times, with many younger men having greater awareness.

Mostly, however, any such departure from tradition is spoken of as *helping* – the inference being that it is men *helping* women. This implies that running a household is really women's work. Usually, there is no thought given to this implied meaning and the effect it can have.

Not long ago, I was the guest speaker at a Rotary Club. The first thing I did was to ask the men there to put up their hands if they helped at home. They all put up their hands.

There was one woman there, and I asked her when she is doing domestic duties, does she think about it in terms of helping, and of course she didn't, because when a woman does 'housework' it is never seen as helping or referred to as such.

Often, when men participate in any of these activities, there is an assumption they are being magnanimous or generous, and there is an expectation of acknowledgment, or of a reward – probably sex, in many cases. I believe this is rarely the case for women.

Sometimes women are envious when they observe the partners of their friends participating in household chores or taking care of the children. I have seen some couples as clients where the women have said their friends think they are lucky. Yet their question has been, 'How come I don't feel so good?' No doubt because of their feelings of indebtedness. There can also be a suggestion from the men that they are not like other guys, compounding the feeling of indebtedness, and adding to the delicacy of the situation.

There are men who play no part in parenting or household responsibilities. It is made clear they believe this is the woman's role. Usually they think this is perfectly legitimate.

On one occasion, my partner and I were talking to another couple about cooking. The man said he did none of the cooking, and he thought this was a perfectly reasonable situation. The woman's expression indicated she had no say about this, and she was not happy about it.

Some men pretend they are involved, but they are not. They claim to believe in participating in these activities, but they don't actually participate.

Chapter 5
How to Understand Abuse in Relationships

So what is the problem? How do we make sense of it? I started asking these questions many years ago. There were various ways I tried to make sense of the abuse.

I discovered one way of understanding the problem – as well as some solutions – when I read two books: Simone de Beauvoir's *The Second Sex* (1948), and Kate Millett's *Sexual Politics* (first published in 1969 and more recently in 2000).

Although these books are not recent publications, they have so much to offer in terms of what is relevant for us now. One of the chapters in Millett's book, *The Theory of Sexual Politics*, is an explanation of the problem that can lead to a solution.

This is what I had been looking for. I wanted a way of thinking about the issue that was going to assist me in helping other people.

There is one sentence in the book that switched on the lights for me and I realised this is what I had been searching for. It made sense of so much I had seen and heard about. The sentence reads: 'Those awarded higher status, tend to adopt roles of mastery, largely because they are first encouraged to develop temperaments of dominance' (Millett p. 47). This means that those considered 'superior' or 'better' tend to take control because they are first urged to dominate.

Simone de Beauvoir explained it in *The Second Sex* back in the 1940s:

> Males have always and everywhere paraded their satisfaction of feeling they are kings of creation. 'Blessed be the Lord our God, and the Lord of all worlds that has not made me a woman,' Jews say in their morning prayers ... Among the blessings Plato thanked the gods for was, first, being born free and not a slave, and second, a man and not a woman. ... Religions forged by men reflect this will for domination: ...They have put philosophy and theology in their service, as seen in the previously cited words of Aristotle and St Thomas." (de Beauvoir p.11)

As far as we can go back in recorded history, that being some five thousand years, males have had higher status in most societies. Men have been the masters, the ones to hold power, and rule. In relationships, because men are considered to be better or superior, they control women and hold power over them, by dominating.

This happens when a man allows himself to be influenced by this notion of superiority and needing to maintain it. It is done in the range of ways we touched on earlier, all of which amount to being aggressive, abusive or violent.

When it comes to the family, the man has been regarded as the head of the family, the one who is in charge, the leader. This is the foundation of the institution. It is maintained in most parts of the world. It is supported in the Bible, the contents of which are unquestioned by believers.

The notion that men are in charge in the family is a long-established custom or belief – one that has been handed down from generation to generation. It is embedded in the psyche of most people. We experience and observe it in our environment. It is accepted as being normal.

Millett suggests that this dominant position occupied by the man precedes the notion of being in charge. Consequently, this would suggest that the character traits mentioned earlier – such as the bad temper, anger and moodiness – are the methods used to maintain this position.

The customs in many households are based on the acceptance that men think they can do whatever they want. After all, they *are* the bosses. No one can challenge them.

Of course, if anyone does challenge the men, who knows what might happen? The bad temper, uncontrollable anger, or moodiness might come to the fore. It is seen as much easier to comply.

To reiterate: so-called bad temper, uncontrollable anger and moodiness are none other than ways of showing dominance. Anger is a feeling any of us can experience, and express, without the need to be violent or aggressive. Common usage has tended to equate anger and violence.

I think anger management groups are on the wrong track, as this focus misses the point. What is called anger, or bad temper, is aggression. And this is used to dominate.

Men maintain their position as master of the household. All achieved with ease and grace, and no thought of the effect on the other members of the household, who just have to accept it. Others in the house live in fear of the men, or at least, there is an uneasy atmosphere. Usually nothing is said, and this is how they lead their lives. As awful as it is, some can think they just have to accept it; after all, these men are the husbands and fathers. Often it is not acknowledged until someone outside the family says something.

I want to include some examples here to emphasise the breadth of this issue.

A woman I saw as a client was a successful businesswoman. I will refer to her as Mary. Her husband – let's call him Ken – was a senior public servant. Mary felt like a prisoner with Ken. Whenever she had been out doing anything on her own, he would question her thoroughly when she arrived home.

Mary went to the gym regularly, and after a workout session she would watch her friends go out for coffee together. But she felt she could never join them, as Ken would expect her to be home at a particular time, and he would be wondering where she was if she wasn't home by that time. He would then question her, and insinuate that she must have been having an affair.

That is not an uncommon experience for a lot of women. They are accused of having relationships with other men, when there is no basis at all to the accusation. As a way of explaining this sort of behaviour, some would suggest it is associated with the man's insecurity, or his low self-esteem, or that he is simply jealous. These explanations are not helpful, and this will become clear later in the book.

Mary and Ken had been together as a couple for thirty-five years, and they had two adult sons. And that was the way Ken had treated Mary for the whole time they'd been together. After several counselling sessions, and after finding out more about how Mary felt and what she wanted, I was able to get her to see she had an option of staying with Ken and continuing her life this way, or she had the choice of leaving him. She chose the latter, and was able to get on with her life in a totally different way. It was as if she had never thought she had an option, that this was the way things were in the relationship, and that she just had to accept it.

I should add that during the process of these sessions, the option of having Ken involved as well was discussed, but he did not want to take part. At a much later stage, I did have contact with Mary and Ken in a social context. They had separated at this stage and Ken was quite happy living on his own and getting on with his life. He said he had blamed me for their separation initially, and had made the assumption that I must be a terrible person. However, he ultimately decided that I was okay!

Often when on the receiving end of abuse, people will blame themselves. When Alice came to see me, she explained how her husband Paul treated her and their two young sons.

Paul was not physically violent, but he was abusive in a range of other ways, so much so that he was like a tyrant in the home. Alice did not tell me he blamed her, although very early on in that session I'd said, 'It has nothing to do with how you are, Alice.' I went on to say some other things, but Alice sat there as if transfixed, not needing to hear anything else.

After sitting there in silence for what seemed like a long time, seemingly in a trance, Alice finally emerged from the daze and said, 'Are you saying it has nothing to do with me?' I reassured her that she was not to blame, and that he was the only one responsible for his actions.

Alice then described how she had been treated for years. She was always told it was her fault, and she was made to feel almost nothing was okay, and that she was to blame for every inconvenience. That is a number of years ago now, and I remember her so clearly, and I'm amazed at how emotional I've become as I write this.

What I said to Alice was all she needed to hear. She was able to make plans from there to get on with her life. These people were middle class, and were seemingly comfortable financially, living in the 'right' suburb.

This also reminds me of an occasion when we were invited to stay overnight with a couple where there is a family connection. On our arrival it was obvious there was tension in the air.

In the evening, the husband Tony went to bed quite early because he wasn't feeling well. When he did, we sat down with Tony's wife, Nancy, and she told us that just before we arrived, he'd thrown a hot cloth at her and hit her in the face.

She then began to tell us many similar incidents had occurred over the twenty years they had been together. It became clear, as she continued, that she believed she was to blame. We emphasised to her that was not the case at all. Again, as with the previous woman, this made all the difference to her, and it was not long afterwards that Nancy and Tony separated.

It is important, I believe, for me to mention one more situation involving some friends of ours. Before they married, Jack had been a friend of mine for a number of years. He and his wife, Andrea, lived fairly close to where we were, and we saw them socially many times.

Whenever we saw them, invariably they would refer to each other using terms of endearment, so everything seemed fine. Several years ago, however, the pair separated. I saw Jack a few times after that, and he said some disgusting things about Andrea. I maintained contact with Andrea, and still do, and she told me an amazing story.

It seems Jack undermined Andrea and put her down constantly during the many years they were together. We have talked about this a number of times when I've seen her, and very often she questions why she stayed with him so long – and she finds this question very hard to answer.

Andrea said there was an occasion, several years before they separated, when she was going to leave, and Jack begged her not to go. I recall her saying he even broke down and cried. Jack and Andrea have three adult children, and he treated them badly as well, and they want nothing to do with him. Jack no longer has contact with me, which I'm pleased about, given what I now know.

I felt the need to include this here, as I think it is an important indication of the pervasiveness of this issue. You are likely to encounter this anywhere, possibly at times when you would least expect it.

These days there is so much focus on terrorism in the world, and how we have to be alert to this possibility. Billions of dollars are being spent on our protection. But terrorism in the home occurs throughout the world and barely rates a mention. Little money is spent on it. It is a hidden problem and far more common than most people think.

So, to summarise … anger management is not the key to an extraordinary relationship between a woman and a man. Managing, repressing, suppressing anger is not the answer. Issues with anger are not the real problem. What is needed is a complete overhaul of men's attitudes of superiority over women. Once they see that there are many ways to think and act, not just their way, and that they have no innate right to feel superior, there can be a realisation of the importance of a freedom for mutual appreciation to gain harmony in an intimate relationship.

Chapter 6
Other Outcomes

With most couples I saw as clients, I observed an imbalance in their relationships. There were two levels, the upper level and the lower. Men were on the former, and women on the latter. I saw it so often I called it 'the same old story'.

Earlier I mentioned the way women say: 'He never listens to me.' It is a comment one hears repeatedly. It seemed as if the men could have been saying: 'We don't have to listen to you. Who do you think you are? You're not on our level.'

Men are not actually saying or thinking this, but their behavior often implies it. It is a manifestation of seeing themselves on a higher level than women.

The men spare no thought about what it is like for women to come up against these views, as they believe women's feelings are not worth considering, since they are inferior and don't matter.

Women are also accused of 'nagging'. Could this be they are not being listened to, and when they repeat themselves, they are accused of nagging to be put back in their place? How often is the term 'nag' or 'old nag' used to describe women? Are men ever described this way?

It is not only within relationships that women are not listened to, but in other situations as well, such as social gatherings. Women will testify to this, and when one is aware of it, it is not difficult to notice.

When men listen to women, they are acknowledging them, and relating to them as an equal. I recall an occasion with a client, when, after looking at these issues, he came back for another session, and said how amazed he was at what his partner had to say. He acknowledged he had never really listened to her before.

Feminist authors Shere Hite and Kate Colleran wrote a book entitled *Good Guys, Bad Guys And Other Lovers: Every Woman's Guide to Relationships* (1990), which gives voice to many women speaking about their experiences of men not listening. Here is one example.

One woman remembers a type of non-conversation she had in college:

> Don was very kind and loving, but he didn't think that what women had to say was nearly as important as what men had to say. We would be hanging out at parties with his friends and some of mine, and the conversation would go something like this: Guy 1: Yo, Donny, we nailed 'em. (Making a crude victory gesture and then

putting Don in a half-nelson.)

Guy 2: Yeah, you didn't save that too brilliantly, did you Don?-

Guy 1: Hey, Don, wanna beer? Candy, wanna beer? (Don kisses me on the cheek and asks me if I want a beer as he's walking away. I realise it doesn't matter what I say, I'm going to get a beer whether I want one or not. He assumes I want what he wants.)

Guy 2: Candy, where'd you get that hat? (Tweaking the brim of my hat and pinching my cheek as one would a little baby.)

Guy 3: That's a weird hat. I don't mean weird, I've just never seen one before. (This is said without looking at me, sort of glancing around.)

Me: It's from the shop in Northampton that sells hats and gloves, you know... (I look at him as I say this, but realise the question was not meant to be answered. Silence ...)

Guy 1: Hey, Don, you going to the Christmas party?

Don: Yeah, Candy and I are going.

Me: When is that? (No one answers me. I am now beginning to feel like jumping up and down and waving my hands in their faces so they take notice. Hello! H-E-L-L-O!)

Guy 2: I'm taking Melissa.

Guy 1: Melissa Capen?

Guy 2: Yeah ...

Guy 1: You're kidding! She's a bit of all right ... I gotta go... I have Professor Valentine in the morning and we have an exam on the fundamentals of American Constitutional Law ...Me: I took that last year ... He usually asks you questions on –Guy 2: Sam told me it's all on the first section of the green text.Me: Uh, I'm trying to tell you – (Small beads of sweat are now forming on my temples and upper lip.)They all collectively decide that the conversation is over – and it is clear if they were asked to recollect it later, they probably "would not remember that I was there". (Hite and Colleran, p.6)

In their book, the authors write about how many women feel so lonely when in a relationship, more lonely than if they were on their own. One woman states:

'During the last relationship I had with a man I spent moments so lonely I sometimes wondered if everyone else had disappeared off the face of the earth. I am so glad I have finally divorced him and started my life again because I felt so incredibly alone when we were married. Isolated. Ignored'. (Hite and Colleran, p.27)

The authors go on to say that:

One of the most common, yet unnamed, causes of fights in relationships is emotional battering or emotional violence. The atmosphere these attitudes create, built as they are into the language

44

about women – and into 'trivial' everyday behaviour towards women – forms the background against which most relationships are lived. This frame of reference can create so much tension, defensiveness and discomfort that many single women even try to avoid getting involved in new relationships. (Hite and Colleran, p.30)

It is a very big statement to say: '... forms the background against which most relationships are lived'. And yet I believe it is true. I know Hite and Colleran's book was written some time ago, nevertheless it is likely that the situations described within its pages are still widespread today.

Reading these accounts has a big impact on me. I feel sad that so many women have led such miserable lives, and I am appalled at the thought of how many women still live this way.

While on the subject of 'listening', I'd like to quote Adele Horin, who was working as a columnist for the *Sydney Morning Herald* when she noted 'a shortage of men that women can relate to. The crisis in male-female conversation cries out for more attention. Relationships are being destroyed, or aborted at first date ...' (Horin, 2008).

Horin continued:

Say a woman has found a man ... Before long she has detected the fatal flaw. "He just doesn't listen. He won't talk to me." She thinks it is an individual problem, and that a more sympathetic conversational mate can be found ... But this conversational crisis is bigger than any individual. It is gender-wide. And it starts young. (Horin, 2008).

'Boys imitate the modelling of other men,' she says, '... boys – with exceptions of course – soon develop the minimalist style mothers, girlfriends and wives despair of.' (Horin, 2008)

I've expanded on this elsewhere, by indicating that if we as males see ourselves as superior, this places men on a higher level and women on a lower level. Given this structure, many men will not allow themselves to feel equal to women – for if they are not superior, they believe that it follows that they will be inferior.

The situation is like a competition, as it is win/lose, with men assuming that: 'If I'm not in charge, or on a higher level, then she will be. Then I will be on a lower level and she will be in charge, and it's not supposed to be like that.'

For a lot of men it is paramount to demonstrate how the proper structure is in place. What better way of doing this than not listening, or taking any notice of women.

As I've said, having been a counsellor for many years, I came across this situation with couples on a regular basis. I encountered it so often I came to refer to it, as I indicated earlier, as 'the same old story'.

Often, it is thought there are communication problems between couples. Lots of professionals respond by teaching their clients skills, without any reference to this imbalance. But teaching skills will not help – not if the imbalance is not addressed.

Men are often accused of lacking empathy, or not having the ability to identify with and understand another person's feelings or difficulties. Because men often function from a position of perceived superiority, this is not surprising.

The comment is often made: 'Don't men realise what effect they are having?' But it follows that if women don't matter, why should men care about how women feel?

There are many examples of this:

- Thinking one can do whatever one wants, regardless of the effects

- Not sharing domestic responsibilities

- Being abusive verbally

- Using intimidating behaviour

- Physical or sexual abuse.

- Child abuse ... and so on.

I saw a number of men as clients who had sexually abused children. They came to see me after they had been 'found out' committing child sexual abuse as adults. They did not come to deal with the problem, they were only pretending.

Their attitude was: 'What's the problem?' There was a lack of remorse, and no thought for the children at all. Their main concern was that they had been 'found out'.

Men who sexually abuse children are often referred to as pedophiles. The inference being that it is a syndrome or disorder, and it is out of their control. But this is not the case, as they are men who choose to sexually abuse children.

This brings us back to the idea of male superiority, which leads to the situation where there is an imbalance in their main relationship. It is possible that one could say this is the case with a large number of couples.

There seem to be very few relationships where people are really satisfied. Yet it would never be thought this is the case, and would be vigorously denied, even scoffed at. There is often a pretence, and an un-awareness that anything else is possible, and people lead unfulfilled lives in ignorance.

One time when I was having a haircut, the barber said to me, 'Do you really think men and women can have a harmonious relationship?' The inference seemed to be that he didn't think it was possible ... yet he *was* married with two young children!

This belief of superiority is firmly embedded in the subconscious of males. That means it is present in our minds without us being aware of it. We can be involved in mental activity that our conscious minds do not recognise is happening. This can influence our behaviour without our knowledge. If we don't analyse this process in order to understand, it is impossible to avoid becoming prey to the programming.

The examination is often resisted for various reasons. One reason is a simple denial that this sense of superiority is there at all. Possibly the major hurdle to overcome is to get beyond the defensiveness, the scoffing, and the denial. If that is achieved, then the mind can be opened. Addressing this is no big deal. It is simply a matter of having this knowledge, and showing it by how we live. It is not complicated.

We tend to think that in order to understand our behaviour, we require some perception or knowledge at a great depth, and this involves processes that are complex and difficult to understand. It can't be easy, people think. It seems too simple to just recognize that this sense of superiority exists and consciously deal with it.

The next barrier can be pride. Surely, if a solution is simple, it should have been realised. Not necessarily. It is often said that the thing most lacking is common sense. Many men are too proud to admit that they've been living with a false idea all their lives.

Getting beyond the idea that men are superior, and therefore in charge and having the right to dominate, can be an easy process. It is simply a matter of men making a decision to accept that they are equal, and similar, to women, and there is no place for anyone to be superior, or in charge, or dominate.

We can start looking at what a difference this attitude makes in our relationships, and how we can have an emotionally close friendship with our partners that most of us have never realised is possible.

However, before we do that, there is another area to explore, an area that also plays a part in creating difficulties in our relationships.

Chapter 7

Differences Between Men and Women

Another subject that plays a significant role in creating difficulties in partnerships between men and women is the idea that we are different. It is in no way exaggerating to emphasise the obstructive qualities associated with such views, and the damaging outcomes that follow.

Unknowingly, so many people are persuaded by these ideas, and are not aware they are connected, with a vested interest in maintaining the status quo. This is a nice subtle way of not upsetting the apple cart!

It is usually made clear this difference is biological. This is the way we are. It is innate, pre-ordained, and accepted as a given. The explanation put forward is that everything was established before we were born and there is nothing we can do about it. It is part of the usual way of thinking and rarely questioned. It is generally thought men are like this and women are like that.

The idea of differences between men and women has been immortalised in the saying: 'Men are from Mars, women are from Venus.'

The inference being that we are so different you would think we come from different planets.

One hears reference to the expression often. If one were to ask any group of people, as I have, it is rare that someone has not heard it. It has become common usage and part of our language. It is usually accepted without question.

Many are not aware the expression originated from the title of a book by John Gray that was first published in 1992, *Men Are From Mars, Women Are From Venus.* The book appeared on the *New York Times* bestseller list in April 1993, and remained there for the next six years.

It has had a big impact on the thinking about the differences between men and women, regardless of the fact there are questions about how Gray arrived at his conclusions. There is no unchallenged scientific evidence available to support his theories.

After all, as Millett, writing as far back as 1969, stated: 'It appears that we are not soon to be enlightened as to the existence of any significant inherent differences between male and female beyond the bio-genital ones we already know. Endocrinology and genetics afford no definite evidence of determining mental-emotional differences'. (Millett, p.50)

Nevertheless, Gray's views concur with the existing state of affairs about these beliefs. We will examine these in the next section.

Before we do that, I want to quote an Amazon review of a book called *The Mismeasure of Woman: Why women are not the better sex, the inferior sex, or the opposite sex,* which was written by Carol Tavris and published in 1992. The review begins with Tavris's seminal statement: 'When man is the measure of things, woman is forever trying to measure up'. (Goodreads: 1993)

The review continues: 'In this enlightening book, Carol Tavris unmasks the widespread but invisible custom – pervasive in the social sciences, medicine, law, and history – of treating men as the normal standard and women as abnormal. Tavris expands our vision of normalcy by illuminating the similarities between women and men and showing that the real differences lie not in gender, but in power, resources, and life experiences.' Let me demonstrate from the following excerpts how Tavris can encapsulate the hidden underlying attitudes stifling relationships:

...when we get into the realm of abilities and qualities – such as doing well in math, the likelihood of roaring at the children, having a sense of humor, needing friends and family, being able to love, or being able to pack a suitcase – the overlap between men and women is always far greater than the difference, if any. (p.42)

Tavris goes on to offer a change in thinking:

Suppose therefore, that we move away from the narrow and limited question of "Do men and women differ, and if so, who's better?" and ask instead: Why is everyone so interested in differences? Why are differences regarded as deficiencies? What function does the *belief* in differences serve? (p.43)

Chapter 8
Nature Versus Nurture

When it comes to differences between men and women there is a belief, based on nature, that these differences are innate. The belief says: This is the way we are born. This is how our makeup is. It was all decided before we were born.

The argument is it has all happened in the processes we go through in the womb. As foetuses are being formed, there are various components that go into the makeup of the male foetus, and different components that go into the female foetus. It is a bit like a production line. This one gets certain items attached to it, and that one gets other items. Or there is certain equipment left out of one that is added to the other.

For males, aggression is added, while emotional and nurturing components are left out. For females, different components – such as passivity, meekness, emotion, nurturing and caring – are added, while aggression is left out.

In reality none of this happens, which highlights the lack of foundation to the belief.

Kate Millett argued that this is a belief, because there is no scientific evidence that makes it clear that there are any differences between males and females before we are born, apart from the bio-sexual ones we all know. (Millett 1969, p.50)

Instead, she says, the apparent differences between men and women are the result of what happens from day one after birth. The process is very thorough and everything is established at a very early stage. It has been suggested that by around eighteen months of age, the identity and the various components of each individual are well-known and established.

Millett covers this so well that I feel compelled to quote precisely what she says:

> Because of our social circumstances, male and female are really two cultures and their life experiences are utterly different – and this is crucial. Implicit in all the gender identity development which takes place through childhood is the sum total of the parents', peers', and the culture's notions of what is appropriate to each gender by way of temperament, character, interests, status, worth, gesture, and expression. Every moment of the child's life is a clue to how he or she must think and behave to attain or satisfy the demands which gender places upon one. In adolescence, the

merciless task of conformity grows to crisis proportions ... one has some cause to admire the strength of a 'socialisation' which can continue a universal condition 'on faith alone', as it were, or through an acquired value system exclusively. What does seem decisive in assuring the maintenance of the temperamental differences between the sexes is the conditioning of early childhood. Conditioning runs in a circle of self-perpetuation and self-fulfilling prophecy. To take a simple example: expectations the culture cherishes about his gender identity encourage the young male to develop aggressive impulses, and the female to thwart her own or turn them inward. The result is that the male tends to have aggression reinforced in his behaviour, often with significant anti-social possibilities. Thereupon the culture consents to believe the possession of the male indicator, the testes, penis, and scrotum, in itself characterises the aggressive impulse, and even vulgarly celebrates such encomiums as 'that guy has balls'. The same process of reinforcement is evident in producing the chief 'feminine' virtue of passivity. (Millett, pp.53-54)

As she explains, in much contemporary terminology, temperamental traits are divided along the misguided lines of 'aggression is male' and 'passivity is female'. 'All other temperamental traits are somehow – often with the most dexterous ingenuity – aligned to correspond.' (Millet, pp.53-54)

Socialisation continues in a way that seems to have no end or limit. So much so, that we are led to think the differences occurred before we are born. Or that they are based on nature, or are innate.

It is thought to be correct because of the way we see boys and girls behaving in a consistent manner. We hear expressions that indicate what we expect of each sex. 'That's how boys are', and 'That's how girls are'. This is a given, it's natural. There is no suggestion it is an outcome of a process we have been through.

People have held the view that these differences are based on nature for a long time. Many would regard not accepting this belief as ridiculous, and be very opposed to such a suggestion.

There's a quote attributed by many to the philosopher, Arthur Schopenhauer, which says that truth passes through three stages.

First, it is ridiculed. Second, it is violently opposed. Third, it is accepted as being obvious. There was a belief – one that was firmly in place, and that had been universally accepted for thousands of years, up until the time of Galileo in the 16th century – that the earth was flat. Galileo caused great controversy when he claimed the earth was not flat. He was accused of being a heretic, and was threatened with being burnt at the stake. Galileo withdrew his claim to avoid such a fate. (Schopenhauer, p.451)

Nevertheless, after that time, it became accepted that the earth is not flat. Be that as it may, I discovered there are people who belong to a Flat Earth Society. They have a website and a newsletter: (http://www.theflatearthsociety.org/home/index.php)

The length of time that the planet Earth was thought to be flat held sway in people's continuing acceptance of it as being flat. It is unreasonable to accept the belief of differences between men and women being based on nature, if there is no factual foundation to the belief. Nor is there any need to accept this conviction due to its longevity.

Studies have failed to come up with any firm conclusion about differences between men and women based on nature as mentioned earlier. Authors like Gray and others who focus on differences, make no reference to studies to prove this. They write as if this is fact.

In my view this belief has contributed to difficulties couples experience, as it becomes a reference point for having a vested interest in maintaining the status quo.

It has occurred to me that an almost absolutely rigorous process, usually referred to as the scientific method, is required before a phenomenon, whose cause or explanation is in question, is able to be accepted. Anything less than that is generally rejected out of hand, as it is considered there is no benchmark to judge the validity of whether it is logically or factually sound.

Let's take a look at what Tavris has to say about 'differences' based on scientific research.

> It seems curmudgeonly to sound words of caution, but the history of brain research does not exactly reveal a noble and impartial quest for truth, particularly on sensitive matters such as sex and race differences. Typically, when scientists haven't found the differences they were seeking, they haven't abandoned the goal or their belief that such differences exist; they just moved to another part of the anatomy or a different corner of the brain. (Tavris p.44)

In other words, the world of science has been dominated by men, and men have pursued their make-based ideas and come up with answers that suit their prejudices:

Yet, here we have a system that has been in place for at least as long as recorded history, as we have known no other, and there has been no scientific method assigned to establish its validity.

The structure I am making reference to is that in which males have higher status. The absurdity of the situation is such that most in the higher position don't even want to think about explanations or causes. There is no reasonable way of achieving such a conclusion, and so it is simply a belief that has been arrived at without any proof. It has mythical overtones, as it is a mistaken belief.

The consequences of such a way of thinking, some of which we are touching on here, are very far-reaching and inevitably disastrous. The good news is that this structure, which has been in place for so long, and which for most of that time has not been questioned, can all be changed, and the consequences are awesome.

The great news is that changing our perspective to one that acknowledges no differences between men and women based on nature, leads us to find out what benefits there are for us from accepting this discovery.

I will get to this later. First, there are other details related to this notion of difference that we need to consider.

Chapter 9
Other Ways Women Are Regarded

There are many ways women are referred to that reinforce the idea of differences between men and women. Often these differences are not flattering to women; many are put-downs.

An example is the assertion that women talk more than men, and figures are mentioned to 'support' this. Karl Kruszelnicki, in his book *Please Explain*, makes the point that, 'A statement said often enough can take on a life of its own. How about this one? "Women speak 20,000 words a day, but men speak only 7,000"'. (p.177)

It fits with all the clichés that television sitcoms and popular pseudo-psychology books spread so effortlessly. You hear it all the time. And it has zero truth.

He mentions several people who make these claims, and finds it telling that the numbers vary so much. One says women speak 50,000 words a day, and men only 25,000. Another has men at 2,000-4,000, and women at 6,000-8,000. There are several other figures mentioned that differ from these.

Kruszelnicki states that, 'the research that has been done tells us there is no gender difference in the number of words spoken.' He quotes other researchers, stating: 'It is shown that the widely held belief that women talk more than men is unsupported in the literature.'

He also mentions a claim by Allan and Barbara Pease who conclude that 'women are four times more likely to suffer from jaw problems'. But Kruszelnicki writes that the authors refer to no study to support their claim. (p.179)

Another aspect that is brought up is the difference between the male and female brain as an indication of the differences between the sexes. In *Please Explain*, reference is made to the book *The Female Brain,* written by Louann Brizendine, when Kruszelnicki observes that,

> This book was roundly criticised in the science journal *Nature*. The reviewers of her book wrote: *The Female Brain*, disappointingly, fails to meet even the most basic standards of scientific accuracy and balance. The book is riddled with scientific errors ... [and] the text is rife with 'facts' that do not exist in the supporting references. (2007, p.178)

It is interesting to note the many words, expressions, and references used to describe women. Significantly, these words and expressions do not portray women in a positive light. Examples include: ball and chain; she who must be obeyed; 'er inside; trouble and strife (cockney rhyming slang for wife); whore; slut; bitch; nymphomaniac; and the enemy ... not to mention all those references to blondes being dumb.

There are no similar terms used to describe men. On the contrary, for example, young men in particular who may have a number of sexual relationships, are referred to as taking actions such as 'sowing wild oats' with no negative connotations. It is perfectly acceptable.

Why are women called girls? Girls are children, or young people. They are not adults. Isn't this demeaning to women? Isn't it another subtle way of putting women down, or on a lower level than men?

Men are not called boys, as women are called girls, even in many regular situations, rather than just sporting environments. At a family gathering I attended, one of the men mentioned he had to sack a girl at work for some reason. This was not something which had been discussed among us previously, however another man there asked, 'You mean woman, don't you?' Had it been a male person in question, the first man would not have referred to him as a boy. The woman was aged 40. In my view, the equivalent terms are man and woman, not man and girl.

This practice of demeaning women through the choice of language is widespread and used by women as much as men. It has simply become common usage, without any thought to its implications.

Another example of differences involves women often being referred to in terms of their role as mother, or grandmother. This does not happen in relation to men.

When Julia Gillard was Deputy Prime Minister of Australia, she had her capacity to hold such an office brought into question by men who accused her of being deliberately barren, and as a non-parent, therefore, unqualified to run the country. (https://en.wikipedia.org/wiki/Bill_Heffernan) Would a man's capacity to hold office be brought into question if he were not a parent?

Successful women are regularly exposed to scorn and ridicule. Their looks are commented on, as are the colours and styles of their hair, what they wear, and how they sound. Julia Gillard and Hillary Clinton are good examples of women to whom this happens. I feel this doesn't happen to the same extent with men.

There is criticism that may not be stated directly, that a woman's success makes her somehow less feminine, while a man's success confirms his masculinity.

There is a belief that there is no discrimination in the workplace and women are now on equal terms with men. Yet a Sydney newspaper report in 2008 by the Industrial Relations reporter, Andrew West, showed that:

Some of Australia's top women executives are earning only half the income their male counterparts are pocketing, a new study by the

Federal Government's equal employment watchdog has found.

While women working full-time generally earn 84 per cent of the male wage, a study of top earners in ASX 200 companies, conducted by the Equal Opportunity for Women in the Workplace Agency, found a huge disparity for women in second-tier corporate jobs.

Female chief operating officers and chief financial officers are taking home about 50 per cent of the median wage of their equivalent male co-workers.

The salaries of female chief executives – and the report finds that, among the 200 listed companies, there are just six – and they are on two-thirds of the equivalent male salaries.

'This raises new questions about the gender pay gap,' the federal Minister for the Status of Women [at the time], Tanya Plibersek, told the Herald.

'We used to explain away the pay gap by saying women worked in different industries where the pay was traditionally lower or that they had work patterns broken by child rearing or family responsibilities. But this research suggests we no longer have those excuses.'
(*SMH*, 25 January, 2008)

The study found that the median salary for a male chief executive was $1,395,540 and for a female chief executive $945,252.

West added that, 'Only 3 per cent of chief executives, 5 per cent of production chiefs, 6.5 per cent of chief financial officers, 7 per cent of business strategists and 16 per cent of information technology heads were women'.

By 2016, there hadn't been much change. Nassim Khadem, Deputy Editor of the Business Day section of *The Sydney Morning Herald*, wrote that:

Australian women earnt about 83 cents for every $1 a man earns, according to a new report analysing the gender pay gap. The report by recruitment firm, Glassdoor, titled *Demystifying the Gender Pay Gap*, is based on more than 534,000 salary reports held by the firm on the pay differences between men and women in countries including Australia, the United States, Britain, France and Germany. (*SMH* March 24, 2016)

The Australian results, based on information on more than 4000 local employee salaries, showed that when variables such as age, education, experience, occupation, industry, location, year, company and job title, are taken into account, the adjusted gender pay gap shrinks from 17.3 per cent to 3.9 per cent. More than one-third (38 per cent) of the unadjusted pay gap is explained by differences in how men and women sort into different occupations and industries with varying earning potential.

Figures released last year by the Workplace Gender Equality Agency said men earn on average $27,000 more than women every year. It estimates that the Australian gender pay gap is roughly 17.9 per cent.

(June 4, 2016)

As I was researching this book, I came across the following article by Eamonn Duff with the headline: 'Christmas parties not so jolly for women'.

SYDNEY Christmas parties are getting out of control and women are the victims.

Counsellors have been shocked by an increase in calls as the festive season reaches its peak. This month, three people have called the NSW Rape Crisis Centre hotline every 48 hours to detail rape and indecent assaults at Christmas parties and end-of-year drink functions.

It's happening in factories, offices, law firms, in banks and in high-profile companies we all know," said NSW Rape Crisis Centre manager Karen Willis.

It's not just occurring at parties. Many employees get asked to stay back late this time of year to do overtime. Opportunistic bosses in particular are exploiting this situation. Complaints were rolling in "much earlier and at a higher rate," compared to last year, she said.

Last Christmas, the centre dealt with at least four employment-related sexual assaults each week, 72percent of which were committed by senior managers and company owners. Only 11percent of those victims later lodged formal complaints with police. Ms Willis said: "One of the common concerns relayed to counsellors by victims is that if they take it further, they'll get the sack".

The Sun-Herald has obtained edited transcripts of complaints made to the 24-hour hotline in the past few days and last Christmas.

A 37-year-old Sydney woman told last week how her boss "grabbed her" and tried to push her to the floor after an on-site Christmas party.

"He called me shocking names and said I had teased him all year. I can still feel his hands. I cannot talk to anyone; if my husband finds out, he'll kill him," she said.

Another woman went out for drinks with colleagues and returned to the office to pick up Christmas presents, only to discover she had been followed back by her boss who assaulted her.

"I worked with him for six years. I know his wife and kids," the woman said.

A 28-year-old woman told how a manager who lives in premises off the office "pulled me into his room and threw me on the bed. He then told some of the men who worked on the floor that I had slept with him for money and that they should 'have a go".'

Ms Willis said: "It's common for offenders to cover their tracks after the event by going out of their way to degrade the victim".

Improved confidence in the legal system was prompting women to come forward, but Ms Willis said reported cases were the "tip of the iceberg". (The Sydney Morning Herald, December 16, 2007)

I was not going out of my way to find this information. It just happened to be there in the papers of the moment. One doesn't have to look far to find examples of discrimination against women. Yet there is a common view that everything has changed, and things are fine for women now.

This attitude may well be one of the chief obstacles to making further progress. In conflicts and wars, an integral part of what happens is that women and girls are raped. This is hardly an indication of any change.

In another article headlined: 'Gang rape used as weapon of war in Congo', mention was made that one in five of a group of 11,700 women had been gang-raped or tortured'. (The Sydney Morning Herald, March 8, 2008) What has changed? The same kinds of reports are coming out of war-ravaged Syria, Iraq and many countries involved in warfare over the past few years. ('Syria Has Massive Rape Crisis' http://www.the-atlantic.com/international/archive/2013/04/syria-has-a-massive-rape-crisis/274583; 'Iraq: ISIS Escapees Describe Systematic Rape'https://www.hrw.org/news/2015/04/14/iraq-isis-escapees-describe-system-atic-rape; ' 'Mass Rape, a Weapon of War, Traumatizes South Sudan' http://www.nytimes.com/2016/03/12/world/africa/un-reports-systemat-ic-rape-in-south-sudan-conflict.html?_r=0)

Chapter 10

The Subconscious and the Part It Plays

I want to mention the subconscious, because we are influenced by it without thinking or using our conscious minds. It is important to be aware of the part it plays, and how it takes everything on board without question.

We reason with our conscious minds, but our subconscious minds just accept everything and we can operate automatically from the information stored there.

A good example of this is driving. When we are learning to drive we have to concentrate on everything we need to do to be able to drive. Once we learn to drive, we drive automatically from the information stored in the subconscious.

Our subconscious has stored everything we have experienced from the very beginning of our existence. Everything is there, firmly implanted. If we allow our subconscious minds to run our lives, they will do this for us.

The subconscious is like a vast garden bed. If left unattended, it will sprout huge weeds like we see on building sites that have been left vacant for a long time.

All the ideas, beliefs and attitudes that I have mentioned are firmly implanted in the subconscious. They have been fertilised by what we continue to see and hear. This includes the modelling we get from our parents, as well as the influence of other adults.

We will be affected by these influences, if they are harmful, unless we make conscious decisions to change the data.

The information stored on the hard drive of our computers is not going to change spontaneously. It is the same for us in relation to our subconscious minds.

If we haven't thought about the negative impact some of these ideas can have, and if we haven't chosen to reject them, they can continue to play their part in ruling our lives.

For men, I am referring to the beliefs about being superior, or better than, and in charge of, women – the beliefs about being the boss and having the right to dominate.

For women, I am talking about the acceptance of being secondary, less than, and dutiful – and also the acceptance of being controlled.

There is also the concept that men must never be seen to be 'under the thumb', or have women being seen as 'wearing the trousers' and therefore in charge. There is also the notion that men and women are enemies involved in a battle.

Lots of people pretend. On the surface everything looks okay, but it's not really. There are numerous couples that live their lives in a certain way, and neither partner is really happy. They don't know how things could be different and they lead their lives unsatisfied out of ignorance.

If we don't understand, and therefore change the negative programming, we will continue to be influenced by it. We will also fall prey to the ongoing browbeating and remain stuck being dissatisfied.

The good news is that in the way we decide what programs are on our computers, we can also decide what data we have on the hard drives of our minds, which is our subconscious.

But just with our gardens, where the weeds have to be dug up and replaced with whatever we want to grow there in their place, so it is with our subconscious.

What I have written about is the programming we have received. Unless we dig it up and replace it, we will continue to be controlled by it.

For example, Tavris writes that, 'thinking of the sexes as opposites implies that women and men invariably act in opposition to one another'.

It implies an underlying antagonism or conflict, the pitting of one side against the other, one way (which is right and healthy) versus the other's way (which is wrong and unhealthy). Yet nothing in the nature of women and men requires us to emphasize difference and opposition. We can emphasize similarity. (p.92)

The 'battle of the sexes' for example, is an expression ingrained in our subconscious minds. It is used frequently by both men and women. It is accepted as an everyday expression, without any thought to its meaning.

If we let it stay there, we will be influenced by it unknowingly. What is its meaning? The meanings I have found for 'battle' in the Oxford Dictionary of English are:

Noun:

1. A large-scale fight between armed forces involving combat between armies, warships, or aircraft.

2. A drawn-out conflict between adversaries, or against powerful forces.

Verb:

1. To fight a battle.

2. To strive or contend in order to overcome or achieve something.

I also found a synonym for battle, and that is: 'to wage war'. In line with this is the term 'enemy'. I watched a rerun of the movie *Four Weddings and a Funeral* recently. I'm sure many of you have seen it. It was a popular movie.

There is a scene towards the end of the movie, where Hugh

Grant's character is at the side of the church, unsure if he is going to go ahead with the wedding. The vicar comes in and calls out to him in a very matter of fact tone: ‚Are you ready to face the enemy?'

Do we regard each other as enemies? Are we adversaries waging a war, where we are involved in a drawn-out conflict striving to overcome or achieve something? What is the likelihood of anyone having a successful relationship while being influenced by these ideas and beliefs? Is it possible for enemies who are waging a war against each other to have loving, caring and mutually satisfying connections with one another?

I know it will be said that these ideas are expressed in a playful and joking manner, and that they are not to be taken seriously. Yet I also know that when men use sexist language, or sexually harass women, this 'we're just joking' attitude is used as a common defence as well.

'When women react to being sexually harassed, a comment often made is 'Can't you take a joke?' Women are then made to feel that they are being a spoilsport, as if there is something wrong with them.

What is the solution? I will get to that shortly. Before I do, let's look at the impact of the inferior status of women in other areas, such as countries in the developing world'.

Chapter 11

A Major Impact of Gender Inequality

The unthinking acceptance of gender inequality has far-reaching consequences, with impacts felt in societies all over the world.

One person who has a universal view with direct experience of how serious these impacts can be is Joan Holmes, an American psychologist who was the founding president of the Hunger Project.

Holmes' presentation to the Microsoft Women's Conference in Sydney in 2006 was so all-encompassing, I'd like to spend this chapter on her outline of the link between world hunger and gender inequality.

She stated that about a decade earlier she had come to fully understand what the underlying cause of hunger really was.

'It is something not at all obvious,' she said. 'But something so built into society and so hidden that it takes a long time just to have the facts of the situation reveal themselves. What it is, is gender inequality.'

Former UN Secretary-General Kofi Annan has said: 'Gender equality is more than a goal in itself, it is a precondition for meeting the challenge of reducing poverty, promoting sustainable development and building good governance.' (http://www.brainyquote.com/quotes/quotes/k/kofiannan401690.html)

At the women's conference, Joan Holmes set out a challenge to participants. 'So, let's examine the condition of women and girls in the developing world,' she said.

So, this is what I've learned principally from her on the subject – the facts. When people talk about poverty and hunger what they are really talking about are women and children in suffering. Holmes continues:

The vast majority of the world's poor are women. And the gap between women and men caught in the cycle of poverty has continued to widen in the past decade. An estimated eighty per cent of the world's refugees are women and children. And today, HIV/AIDS is rapidly becoming a women's disease. In several southern African countries, more than three quarters of all young people living with HIV are women.

There is a direct correlation between women's low status, the violation of their human rights, and HIV transmission. There is a growing recognition that gender discrimination is de-humanising and holds back the development of society. What we're not aware of – what we fail to understand – is that gender discrimination, in and of itself, is often fatal.

The cumulative impact of gender bias claims a horrific and incomprehensible number of female lives. Did you know that one hundred million women and girls are 'missing'? Missing from the world's population because of sex-selective abortion, female infanticide, malnutrition, abuse and neglect. This is roughly equivalent to all the deaths in all the wars of the twentieth century, the most violent century ever. This is a holocaust many times over.

In our world community, an horrific number of females die because the gender bias goes largely unnoticed. These women and girls die the same way they lived. Ignored, anonymous, in silence. We need to tell the truth. We still live in a planet where the majority of women live in countries where women are subjugated, abused and abandoned.

And here's the irony: the oppressed, malnourished, and often illiterate women are the key to the future. They are the key to the end of hunger and abject poverty. They are the key to healthier societies, to faster economic growth and to greater social justice.

Holmes says that there are three ways women make a difference:

- in the 'inextricable link between women's well-being and the overall health of a society'

- in the 'largely unrecognised' contribution of women to the world economy

- and 'an unparalleled benefit to society when they have a voice in decisions that affect their lives'.

Holmes explains it better than most people could – in brief: 'Women work two-thirds of the world's working hours, earn one-tenth of the world's income, and own less than one per cent of the world's property'.

She explains that when we say we want to empower women, what we mean is that we want to remove the shackles and constraints that 'control, diminish and dehumanise their lives':

> There's now universal agreement that the single most important intervention for development is the education of girls. Nothing empowers a woman's voice like education. And when women have voice in their villages, they alter the development agenda to address the critical issues of meeting basic needs. … Empowered women begin to transform gender relations and call into question the deeply entrenched patriarchal system.

There is an inevitable conclusion, according to Holmes, which is supported by study after study around the world, and that is that when women are empowered, all of society benefits. These benefits include:

- faster economic growth

- increased agricultural production

- less corruption in governance

- lower malnutrition

- lower child mortality

- more children in schools (including girls)

- greater social justice

- and that the overall health and wellbeing of a society is greatly improved.

Holmes describes gender discrimination as 'the greatest moral challenge of our age'. Despite the overwhelming statistics, her final remarks were upbeat:

As you become better educated on this issue, always – always – share what you are learning. What's needed is social transformation – catalysed by awareness. Do this and you will contribute to ending hunger, ending abject poverty, and ending the worst human rights violation in history. (Holmes, 2008)

Chapter 12

The Sexual Outcomes of an Unbalanced Relationship

Another outcome we need to look at in relation to the notion of being superior is to examine what happens sexually in a relationship. When it comes to sex, it is often only the man's needs that are considered. It is most likely this happens in many sexual relationships between men and women.

Almost universally, there's a focus on the man having an orgasm during intercourse for it to be considered a success. This is the 'Hollywood' portrayal of sex and it is viewed as normal. It is considered that women's needs are met in these circumstances.

As the penis needs to be stimulated to achieve orgasm for men, the equivalent organ for women is the clitoris. There is debate about whether the walls of the vagina are endowed with the necessary sensitivity to generate a female orgasm. Even though a lot of men are not concerned one way or the other, many think this is all that is necessary for female orgasm.

It is common for women to fake orgasms, I would imagine, to fit in with this view. In fact, many women have been led to believe this is how they should have orgasms as well. And if they don't, they can believe there is something wrong with them. Often men have this expectation and if women don't 'come', they can make women feel there is something wrong with them.

I recall when I worked in a sexual difficulties clinic some years ago, the most common issue we dealt with was women who do not experience orgasms. Invariably, all of these women had sought help from other advisers such as doctors, psychiatrists and other therapists – and they had not received the knowledge they required.

Part of the problem was that women generally did not know how to arouse themselves as they had been discouraged from doing this. There was a view that it was not acceptable to be touching oneself 'down there'. One would think this problem is currently not as widespread as it used to be, but it is likely there are remnants.

So with some women, if they don't know themselves, they would be unable to inform their partners about what they would like.

Lots of men are ignorant about women's sexuality, and as already stated, think the woman's needs are met when the man is sexually satisfied during intercourse. Many are not concerned anyway as they are only interested in their own needs. The old cliché about women having headaches probably describes a means by which women avoid having sex because there is nothing in it for them. The feeling of being used would be an additional reason for having this excuse.

What happens in many relationships is that the sex that actually takes place is rape.

This can happen in several ways. One way is simply that many men have the belief that when they are in a relationship, and particularly if they are married, they have a right to expect sex. The woman is meant to realise this and 'come across', as it were, whenever the man wants to have sex. (As indicated earlier with Julie Ramage, that is how it was for her, and she was raped on a daily basis.)

There was a time when there was no law against rape within marriage. Can you believe that rape within marriage was legal? There is such a law now, but I am not aware of anyone ever having been prosecuted.

Women can also be in a double bind. If they show interest, or take the initiative in any way, they can be thought of in negative terms by some men.

A lot of men think women are not meant to take the lead with sexual activity and that it is men who should do that. Women who initiate sex can be regarded as sluts, whores, promiscuous or loose. When this happens, men may not wish to continue, and women are left up in the air feeling confused, thinking the men have lost interest in them.

Naomi Wolf in her book *Promiscuities: A Secret History of Female Desire* (1997) has written extensively about the benefits to be gained by having a better understanding of women's sexuality. This knowledge is so different from the existing state of affairs in relation to the awareness of most men and women in this regard, given that so much focus tends to be on men's sexuality.

Having a relationship on equal terms opens up a whole new arena for mutual satisfaction in regard to people's sexual activity.

Wolf also highlights that this information is not new, and she quotes several authors at length. One is Helen E. Fisher, author of *The Sex Contract: The Evolution of Human Behaviour*, who wrote:

> The human female is capable of constant sexual arousal ... She can make love whenever she pleases. This is extraordinary. No female of any other sexually reproducing species can make love with such frequency ... It was not until the 1950s that investigators documented a second extraordinary human female endowment. Not only is she able to make love with impressive regularity, but her sex organs generate intense sexual pleasure – even more plea-sure than the human male derives from intercourse. For nature has provided the human female with a clitoris, a bundle of nerves designed solely for sex. Furthermore, about four or five dense masses of veins and nerves congregate in the muscles of her gen-

itals – and during intercourse these sensitive aggregates sharply distinguish her sexual performance from that of her mate.

As a woman becomes sexually aroused, blood pours into the vessels of the genitals and the general pelvic area. The nerve bundles begin to expand. The muscles around the clitoris, vaginal opening and the anus begin to swell with blood. Shortly, the spongy sacs that surround the vaginal opening expand to three times their normal size; the inner lips double their size, and the muscles of the entire genital area become engorged with blood.

'For the man,' she writes, 'there are three or four main contractions, a few minor ones, localised in the genital area, and sex is done.'

But the female pattern is different, for women feel five to eight major contractions and then nine to fifteen minor ones. They diffuse throughout the pelvic area. For women, sex may have just begun, unlike her mate, her genitals have not expelled the blood, and if she knows how, she can climax again and again if she wants to. (Fisher 1977 in Wolf 1997, p.168)

Wolf goes on further to discover what the approach to sexuality was in ancient China.

The men of ancient China who followed the Tao were intent on learning how to give their lovers as many orgasms as possible. The Tao view of the preciousness of female desire and all actions that generate and satisfy it is clear in the very language the Taoists used to describe women's anatomy ... The terms the Taoists used to describe women's genitals were metaphors of beauty, sweetness, artistry, rareness and fragrance". (Wolf p.185)

Wolf points out how this is in such contrast to the slang terms of today associated with women's genitals, which are included among the collection of the most foul language in common usage. I prefer not to even mention them, as they are such awful terms, but we all know them.

I find it quite exciting to read what Naomi Wolf has discovered and I have learned a lot.

Now I'd like to share a little of my own situation with you. I have enjoyed a wonderful relationship with Gunilla, my partner of thirty-two years. We have both been married before, and even though we are now married to each other, we prefer to use the term 'partner', as that implies equality.

When we began our relationship, Gunilla had never had an orgasm, even though, apart from being married, she had had several other relationships previously. We have had a thoroughly enjoyable mutually satisfying sexual relationship.

Not long after we met she wrote to me and I will include some of what she said:

I want to tell you how happy I am with you and that meeting you has already had quite an impact on my attitude to life. Basically you have given me hope. I never opened myself to any man before you ... I generally had a fairly low opinion of male members of society, feeling they were not full people somehow. They seemed to lack that special dimension so often found in women: deep and comprehensive insight into human affairs and other issues concerning life, in combination with a desire to preserve and protect instead of being generally destructive.

I know I have started to grow since I met you. I feel a greater control over my life, a widening perspective on my own reflexions. I love and respect you for what you are, a loving, gentle person who can treat other people with integral warmth, kindness and compassion, including women! It is truly difficult to respect people (i.e. men) who don't respect you (i.e. women). How can relationships possibly grow and blossom under unequal conditions? ... the strangest thing I experience for the time being is such strength, unbelievable strength.

Reading now what Gunilla wrote then, I feel a time will come for a better understanding of women's rights. What great insight she displays, particularly in the sentence: 'How can relationships possibly grow and blossom under unequal conditions?'

In the next section we will see how the realisation that men and women are similar makes all the difference to the way we relate to one another, and how this notion allows us to have what amounts to extraordinary relationships.

Chapter 13

How You CAN Have an Extraordinary Relationship

The good news is: you are in charge of yourself.

You are the gardener, responsible for looking after the fertile ground that is your subconscious mind, where everything is planted. It is your choice what you do. You can leave the self-sown seeds of previous seasons in place, allowing them to sprout, producing the same results. Or you can dig up the whole garden, and replace the seeds, so that they will produce a different display.

There's no point in thinking about gender in terms of opposites, and focusing on the differences between men and women, or even the differences between any two people in a partnership.

Author and researcher, Carol Tavris, has something to say about that limited framework of dualism:

Finally, we can resist the temptation to see the world in opposites. Western ways of thinking emphasize dualisms and opposites, and we pose many questions of human life in fruitless either-or terms.

Are we rational or emotional creatures? Will we win or lose? Is this decision good or bad? ... Are we masculine or feminine? As long as the question is framed this way – "What can we do about *them*, the other, the opposite?" – it can never be answered, no matter which sex is being regarded as "them". The question, rather, should be this: What shall we do about *us*, so that our relationships, our work, our children, and our planet will flourish? (p.333)

*

So these are the 10 steps you can take today to begin transforming your relationship.

1. Accept that men and women are on the same level.

We are equally capable. Each is able to achieve efficiently whatever one has to do. Men and women have the same ability.

2. Share leadership in relationships and families.

There is no need to have one person in charge, or accept the belief that the man is the head of the family. Each partner will have the same status, which can lead to a calmness and composure, especially in a difficult situation.

As I mentioned earlier, I once spoke to a group from a church, and before I spoke, the church leader took me aside to let me know the congregation's view about families. He wanted to make sure I realised they believed the man was the head of the family.

When I did speak, among other things, I made it clear there was no need to have one person in charge. Relationships and marriages are *partnerships*. Both partners share the leadership in the family.

In response, many people gave me a standing ovation. Afterwards, a whole group came up to say they had been making this point for a long time, and they were not being listened to.

3. Make decisions jointly

Or make decisions with consideration of the other person, if decisions are made separately. This harmonious approach leads to an air of tranquility within the home environment, with no uncertainty about what is happening, intended, or required.

4. Have mutual respect

Mutual respect can be an established fact, including frequent reciprocated acknowledgement, enhancing the confidence and loyalty experienced by each partner. Can you imagine how that feels on an ongoing basis?

This will mean that women are not seen as secondary, less important, or subservient to men. The need to dominate, or the concepts of honouring and obeying, do not even come into the equation.

5. Listen to one another

The enormous issue of not being listened to, which is an issue experienced by so many women in their relationships, will no longer be a problem, as listening happens naturally. This is a monumental transformation, making such an enormous difference in the lives of a large number of women who would appreciate the encounter.

6. Agree to disagree

Agreeing to differences of opinion is completely acceptable, rather than the common experience of competing, which involves having a winner and loser. Regardless of the outcome, each person is absolutely satisfied.

7. Share responsibility for parenting and household chores

This is an amazing step in the right direction, as this area is one of the major obstacles in so many relationships. In these circumstances, allowances are made naturally and there is no need for resentment.

As indicated at the start of this book, children will benefit immensely having both parents involved in this way. It will make them feel so good about themselves. The modelling they observe will be an example for them to follow, or imitate, enabling them to have great relationships later in life, as well as being exemplary parents. Imagine the astounding consequences resulting from such changes.

The close connection you have with each other is continuously kept alive, and this is a state of being that is not possible in a relationship without equality. This preserves the good feelings between you, resulting in an overall relaxed atmosphere.

8. Be on equal terms

Relating to each other on equal terms means that sexual activity within the relationship becomes a whole new ball game, especially given what we discovered in the previous chapter.

Each person's needs are met, and there are no limitations to exploring what is acceptable in a partnership based on mutual respect and understanding.

As promised at the beginning of this book, you will share all those wonderful attributes that are only possible when you relate to each other as equals, experiencing an air of tranquility associated with the harmony in your life. The friendship, sharing and good communication is guaranteed to delight you both.

9. Enjoy humour

Expressing humour and amusing each other is lots of fun. When there is no conflict, peace based on mental and emotional calm is available to you both. Laughter can dispel worries and, in turn, dispel those worries being projected onto your partner. If you look for humour you can find it at every turn. So why not share it with your loved one?

10. Express your love

The deep affection or love you feel for each other will be unmistakable. Surely this is the grand prize. This is what we all crave, and this is how it can be accessible. It is the most wonderful feeling.

In a letter I wrote to Gunilla, which I have in front of me [Yes, we both wrote to each other!], some of what I said included the words, 'I've never been told the things you have told me by anyone before. My darling Gunilla, I love you and feel very much loved, and I'm feeling great. All my love, Leo.'

This reminds me of a section in John F Schumaker's book, *In Search of Happiness: Understanding An Endangered State of Mind*, in which he quotes a line from Victor Hugo's *Les Miserables*: 'The supreme happiness in life is the conviction that we are loved'.

Schumaker then goes on to say, 'To be is to be loved. In turn, the healthiest forms of happiness are experienced and expressed as love. There are not many sources of happiness that cannot be traced to love. By its highest estimation, love completes us, brings us into harmony, gives us meaning, and binds together all the elements of the universe. In its various forms, love is what human beings do with their need for intimacy. Without intimacy, there is no happiness. Failure to find intimacy will drain the happiness and zest out of a person faster than anything.' (p.216)

Further on, Schumaker writes, 'Love is one of the worst casualties of consumer culture, which finds it difficult to incorporate much genuine love between people into its panacea of work and consumption ...Whereas love was once a power to which one had to surrender, now it

94

is a conscious part of one's life portfolio'. (p.219)

Schumaker's book is a true masterpiece, and even more relevant today than when it was first published in 2006. The main theme of his book is that we have been hijacked by consumerism, and hounded down that path which leads in the opposite direction to happiness. Along the way, trust, loyalty, friendship and connection – which are the essential values of any relationship – have been eroded.

We are constantly being bombarded with the need to have the biggest, best, and latest of everything ... as well as more of everything. This leads to never being satisfied.

I have read and re-read Schumaker's book many times. I have it nearby all the time. It is possible to delve into it anywhere and find real gems. I do this regularly, and when I do, I enjoy an air of serenity. It can be a companion book to the one you are reading.

As I also indicated, as you come to realise that you are in charge of yourself, and you see that to express your love for a partner you now recognize as being on the same level as you, as being your equal, is your greatest opportunity in life for happiness, you will have discovered how to have a relationship that is beyond your wildest dreams. When you experience your relationship in this way, it is like coming up for air. You can take a deep breath, and become familiar with life as you have never done before.

The result is that your life is more fulfilling, richer, more enjoyable and satisfying, providing you with personal reward and great pleasure. Life simply has more meaning.

The result of putting this into practice leads to a peaceful revolution, where the established social order that has been firmly in place for a very long time can be cast aside.

In doing so, a quote attributed to Margaret Mead might sum up a call for action to create your own extraordinary relationship: 'Never doubt that a small group of thoughtful, committed citizens can change the world; indeed, it's the only thing that ever has.' (http://www.interculturalstudies.org)

And regardless of the rest of society and the inequalities that persist between men and women, remember that you are in charge of yourself and your actions. If you strike out to change your world, on your own quest for open communication with, and appreciation of, your partner, then peace, parity and pleasure will be within your reach through the unique qualities of your new-found extraordinary relationship.

References

Annan, Kofi. Kofi Annan quotes http://www.brainyquote.com/quotes/quotes/k/kofiannan401690.html

Brizendine, Louann, 2006, *The Female Brain,* Broadway Books, New York

de Beauvoir, Simone, 1949, *The Second Sex,* Paris

Duff, Eamonn, 2007, *Christmas Parties Not So Jolly for Women,* The Sydney Morning Herald, Dec 16, 2007

Engel, Beverly, *Keynote Speech,* The Truth About Violence Against Women Conference, Sydney, 2008

Gray, John, 1992, *Men Are From Mars, Women Are From Venus,* Harper-Collins Publishers, New York

Hite, Shere & Colleran, Kate, 1989, *Good Guys, Bad Guys, And Other Lovers: Everywoman's Guide to Relationships,* Pandora Press, London

Holmes, Joan, 2006, address to the Microsoft Women's Conference, January 12, 2006, Sydney

Horin, Adele, 2008, 'Listen here, Sonny Jim, and we Might get Somewhere', The Sydney Morning Herald, Sept 6, 2008

Kenworthy, Duncan, 1994, Producer, *Four Weddings and A Funeral*

Khadem, Nassim, 2016, *Gender Pay Gap,* The Sydney Morning Herald, March 24, 2016

Kruszelnicki, Karl, 2007, *Please Explain,* HarperCollins Publishers, Australia

Mead, Margaret, http://www.interculturalstudies.org

Millett, Kate, 1969, *Sexual Politics,* Avon Books, New York

Schopenhauer, Arthur, 1981, *The Harper Book of Quotations,* Collins, London

Schumaker, John F., 2006, *In Search of Happiness: Understanding an en-*

dangered state of mind, Penguin Group (NZ)

Tavris, Carol, 1992, *The Mismeasure of Woman: Why women are not the better sex, the inferior sex, or the opposite sex,* Simon & Schuster, NY

West, Andrew The Sydney Morning Herald

Wolf, Naomi, 1997, *Promiscuities: A Secret History of Female Desire,* Vintage, London

NEWSPAPERS
The Age, Melbourne

The Sydney Morning Herald, Sydney

URLS
http://edition.cnn.com/2013/12/06/us/domestic-intimate-partner-violence-fast-facts/

https://en.wikipedia.org/wiki/Bill_Heffernan

http://www.abc.net.au/news/2014-02-13/mother-in-shock-after-son-killed-by-father-at-cricket-oval/5258252

http://www.abc.net.au/compass/s4502668.htm

http://www.goodreads.com/book/show/692689.Mismeasure_of_Woman

http://www.interculturalstudies.org

http://www.news.com.au/entertainment/tv/matthew-newton-rachael-taylor-in-hotel-lobby-fight-withdraws-channel-seven-show-x-factor/story-e6frfmyi-1225908632404

http://www.smh.com.au/business/workplace-relations/gender-pay-gap-20160322-gnp0vy.html

www.un.org/apps/news/story.asp?NewsID=33971

www.whiteribbon.org.au/white-ribbon-importance

http://www.un.org/es/women/endviolence/pdf/vaw_backgrounder.pdf

Angela's Anorexia:
The story
of my mother

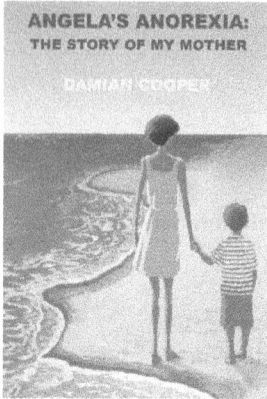

A son's story of the debilitating illness, anorexia nervosa, that his single mother suffered from throughout his childhood. The mother and son formed a close bond and the boy's description of their life together is filled with both joy and sadness. A true story showing the boy's experience of growing up fast in Australia and New Zealand, caring for his mother while coming to understand her sickness and his need to develop an independent spirit early on.

Damian Cooper has written a straightforward, honest and loving account of his boyhood, set against a poignant parallel story of his mother's excessive focus on body image, food, diet and exercise.

Category: SELF-HELP/EATING DISORDERS AND BODY IMAGE

ARCO:
the legend
of the blue vortex

An exciting new story from first-time novelist, **Ferdinando Manzo**, ARCO explores man's battle with the sea in an attempt to seek solace.

The story is set in two different eras: on the high seas among ancient pirates and in contemporary Europe ravaged by war. The legend of the blue vortex – a door into another world – is the central focus of both periods.

An adventure story, it also raises philosophical questions about love and the purpose of life.

Category: FICTION MAGICAL REALISM/ROMANCE/FANTASY

Burma My Mother
And Why I Had To Leave

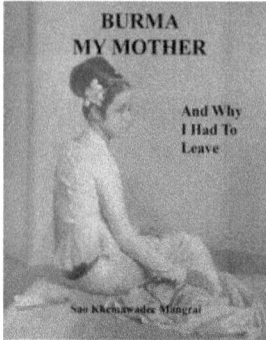

Myanmar's future is informed by its past - and BURMA MY MOTHER tells it like it is.

A valuable story of living through good times and plenty of bad in Burma, now known as Myanmar, before an escape to a new life of freedom.

Author **Sao Khemawadee Mangrai**'s husband, Hom, was imprisoned for 5 years, and his father was shot and killed sitting alongside independence leader, General Aung San, when he was assassinated.

Khemawadee grew up in a Shan state in the north-east of Myanmar, previously known as Burma, and now lives in Sydney. Her sad memories are also infused by the beauty of the country and the grace of Myanmar's Buddhist culture.

Category: MEMOIR

Drenched
by the Sun

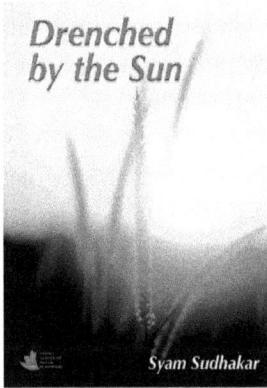

I, who prophesy
by reading the stars and the wind,
now think of that country ...

Syam Sudhakar 'has an eye for the strange and the uncanny and a way of building translucent metaphors,' according to leading South Indian poet, K. Satchidanandan.

An award-winning poet who writes in English and Malayalam, Sudhakar is based in Kerala, teaching and researching Indian poetry.

Category: POEMS

Night Road to Life

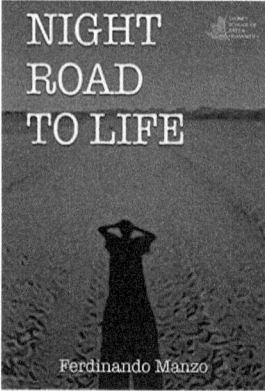

Themes of the sea and the emotions, particularly the deeply felt joys and melancholies experienced by men, are a touchstone of NIGHT ROAD TO LIFE.

Ferdinando Manzo's thoughts are not bound to fluidity; they fly to the greatest heights of exhilaration in poems such as, *The sky above us*, which displays 'a mantle of stars that burns in my heart' and in the evocative lines of *Eclipse*: 'the moon rose, bright between the eyelids of the night'. Even the constellation Andromeda is given due recognition, breaking her chains and ready for revenge, before another poem *The voice of the universe* explores 'a hidden legend as far away as waves in outer space'.

A distinctive quality of this collection of poems is its musicality – the sounds of words carefully chosen, and their rhythms. The pleasing effect of the sensuality of sounds, ranging from gentleness to the drama of sex, is in tune with the gamut of human emotion.

Category: POEMS

Reported Missing

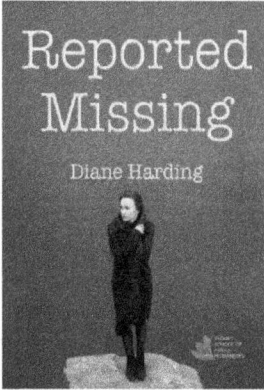

Di Harding's novel is set in a very contemporary Sydney, taking in multi-layered sights and sounds, from the northern beaches to performances at the Sydney Opera House.

The plot spans the complications of what a woman must consider if she is to save her children from domestic violence. And the main character has good reason to hold fears for her life.

What would you do if your daughter was missing and you thought your son-in-law was somehow involved? Is there someone who could help you, or would you take matters into your own hands?

She does, and so the terror begins – from vile and personal harassment to life threatening acts, until she is ready to commit murder.

Her obsession with killing grows in her mind until she begins to plan and plot. Can she actually do it? Then something shocking happens to make up her mind.

The story ends on an upbeat for a new life ahead for the family.

Category: DOMESTIC VIOLENCE/CRIME FICTION/SYDNEY NOVEL/AUSTRALIAN FICTION

Road
to Mandalay
Less Travelled

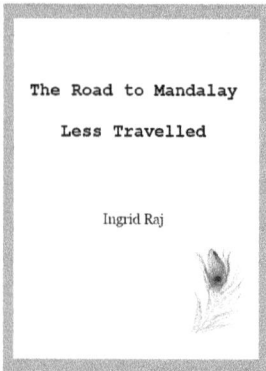

The Road to Mandalay

Less Travelled

Ingrid Raj

'The Road to Mandalay Less Travelled' by **Ingrid Raj** provides research on a selection of Anglo-Burmese writing published from the period of British rule in Burma up until 2007.

What Raj shares with us in this study is the knowledge she gained about the value of social resistance achieved through writing. Both fiction and non-fiction texts are included in arguing a case that these might be viewed as tools of often ambivalent resistance against oppressive regimes, both local and colonial.Her research deserves a wider readership than was initially provided, and to this aim Sydney School of Arts & Humanities presents the work as its first publication in this new category of Essays & Theses.

We hope that specialist researchers as well as members of the general reading public take this opportunity to learn more about the culture of the people of Myanmar through their unique approach to storytelling, based largely on their religious understanding, their rich store of folk legend and their chequered history.

Category: MEMOIR/LITERATURE/BURMA-HISTORY

Road to Rishi Konda

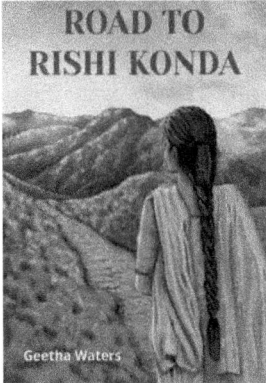

'ROAD TO RISHI KONDA' by **Geetha Waters** is a memoir of insight and charm, with a serious educational purpose. The author recalls delightful and stimulating stories from her childhood to throw light on the work of the philosopher J. Krishnamurti as a revolutionary 20th century educator.

At once fascinating and enchanting, Geetha Waters' stories centre on a girl growing up in Kerala and Andhra Pradesh in the '60s and '70s.

These youthful tales are underpinned by Geetha's deep understanding of childhood education, based both on her academic studies and in practice in her daily life as a mother and childcare professional.

Written from a child's perspective, the tales of awakening to life offer the reader an opportunity to appreciate how all children learn, as they draw on a deep well of curiosity that needs to be respected.

Category: BIOGRAPHY & AUTOBIOGRAPHY
PERSONAL MEMOIR/EDUCATORS

Jiddu Krishnamurti World Philosopher
Revised Edition

The life of the 20th-century philosopher Jiddu Krishnamurti was truly astonishing. As this new updated edition shows, people from all over the world would gather to hear him speak the wisdom of the ages.

Biographer **Christine (CV) Williams** carried out research over a period of four years to write this ebook account of Krishnamurti's life. She studied his major archive of personal correspondence and talks, and interviewed people who knew him intimately.

Krishna was born into poverty in a South Indian village, before being adopted by a wealthy English public figure, Annie Besant. As an adult he settled in California, travelling to India and England every year to give public lectures that inspired spiritual seekers beyond any single religion.

Category: BIOGRAPHY

www.ingramcontent.com/pod-product-compliance
Lightning Source LLC
Chambersburg PA
CBHW071137280326
41935CB00010B/1270